Jonathan Law High School
Teaching & Learning Commons
Milford, CT

COPING WITH

HIV AND AIDS

Elissa Thompson and Paula Johanson

New York

Published in 2020 by The Rosen Publishing Group, Inc.
29 East 21st Street, New York, NY 10010

Copyright © 2020 by The Rosen Publishing Group, Inc.

First Edition

Library of Congress Cataloging-in-Publication Data

Names: Thompson, Elissa, author. | Johanson, Paula, author.
Title: Coping with HIV and AIDS / Elissa Thompson and Paula Johanson.
Description: First edition. | New York : Rosen Publishing, 2020. | Series: Coping | Audience: Grades 7–12. | Includes bibliographical references and index.
Identifiers: LCCN 2018051712| ISBN 9781508187318 (library bound) | ISBN 9781508187301 (pbk.)
Subjects: LCSH: AIDS (Disease)—Juvenile literature. | AIDS (Disease)—Social aspects—Juvenile literature. | AIDS (Disease)—Prevention—Juvenile literature. | AIDS (Disease)—Diagnosis—Juvenile literature.
Classification: LCC RA643.8 .T52 2020 | DDC 614.5/99392—dc23
LC record available at https://lccn.loc.gov/2018051712

Manufactured in China

For many of the images in this book, the people photographed are models. The depictions do not imply actual situations or events.

CONTENTS

INTRODUCTION

A new disease appeared in the early 1980s. It was infecting young homosexual men—and killing them. No one was sure what was happening or why. It was a scary time.

Scientists eventually identified the culprit. They named the disease HIV (human immunodeficiency virus) which, unchecked, turns into the deadly final stage, AIDS (acquired immune deficiency syndrome). They worked hard to learn more about HIV and AIDS and to develop medicine to help. Meanwhile those who received an HIV or AIDS diagnosis struggled, not only with their illness but with the stigma associated with having HIV/AIDS.

Activist Maria Mejia remembers when she was diagnosed at eighteen, in 1991. "The only one that knew was my mother and my little brother," Mejia told Jason Duaine Hahn for *People* magazine. "Though I know she did it to protect me, [my mother] said I shouldn't tell family or friends that I had this, because they would discriminate [against] me."

There was a great deal of secrecy and shame surrounding the disease, partly because HIV can be transmitted through unprotected sex or intravenous

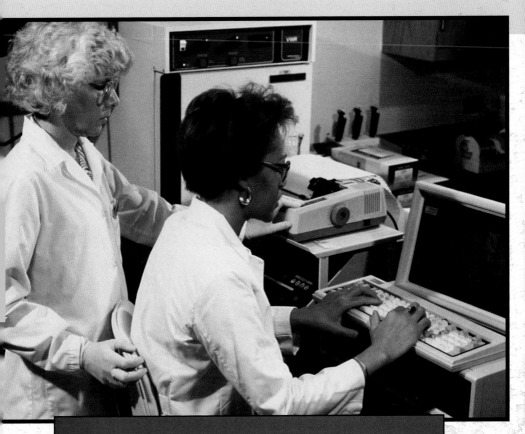

Researchers at the Centers for Disease Control were hard at work in 1988 trying to find the cause of the mysterious disease killing young men.

drug use. People were scared to even sit next to or hug someone with HIV.

In 1991, professional basketball player Magic Johnson announced publicly that he had HIV, shocking many. At the famous press conference he told reporters:

Famous basketball player and philanthropist Magic Johnson shocked the world in 1991 when he announced that he had contracted HIV.

I plan to go on living for a long time. I'm going to be a spokesman for the HIV virus because I want young people to realize they can practice safe sex. Sometimes you're a little naive about it and you think something like that can never happen to you. It has happened but I'm going to deal with it. My life will go on. Life is going to go on and I'll be a happy man.

In 1992, after revealing his HIV-positive diagnosis, Johnson went on to win a gold medal at the Olympics. He proved that even with HIV, you can accomplish so much with your life.

Johnson went on to play basketball in the Olympics and to have three children. Today, he works with the Magic Johnson Foundation to help others.

Much has changed since the 1990s when Johnson and Mejia were diagnosed with HIV. Today, people with HIV can live long lives by taking the correct medicines. Also, doctors now understand how the disease is transmitted so people are better able to protect themselves against contracting HIV.

Still, there is work to be done. Mejia has become an activist, speaking out about HIV and educating others about the disease and how to live with it.

"Just because you got diagnosed with HIV, especially in these times, it does not mean that your life is over," she said. "You can live, you can work, you can thrive, you can survive, you can get married.

"I try to live my life as best that I can. I believe in life, we have choices," Mejia added. "You either put yourself on the bed to die, or you continue to choose to fight, and then when you continue to choose to fight, then you fight for others."

HIV and AIDS can be scary to think about, but the more you know, the safer you'll be.

Numbers Around the World

A lot has changed in the world since the 1980s, when the HIV epidemic began. HIV is still a global concern, but there is hope.

HIV by the Numbers

Here are some statistics about HIV and AIDS from UNAIDS, an organization supported by the Joint Programme in the United Nation and the Centers for Disease Control and Prevention (CDC):

- 36.9 million people around the world were living with HIV in 2017. Of these, approximately 1.2 million live in the United States.
- 38,500 people were infected with HIV in the United States in 2015. Sadly, each year more people become infected with the

virus, and others who were already infected die from AIDS.

- Since it was first recognized in 1981, AIDS has killed 35.4 million people worldwide.
- In the United States, the number of HIV infections is down 8 percent

Right now, there is no cure for or vaccine against HIV. Once you have HIV, you will have it forever. But that doesn't mean there isn't hope. Thanks to therapies that have been developed over the last decade, many people who are currently infected with HIV live longer, healthier lives than did those who first contracted the virus.

HIV/AIDS Explained

So just what are HIV and AIDS? What do they do to the body?

In the 1980s, scientists worked hard to learn more about the mysterious disease. They eventually discovered that HIV is a virus that attacks the body's immune system. The virus destroys CD4, or T cells, which means that the body can't fight off

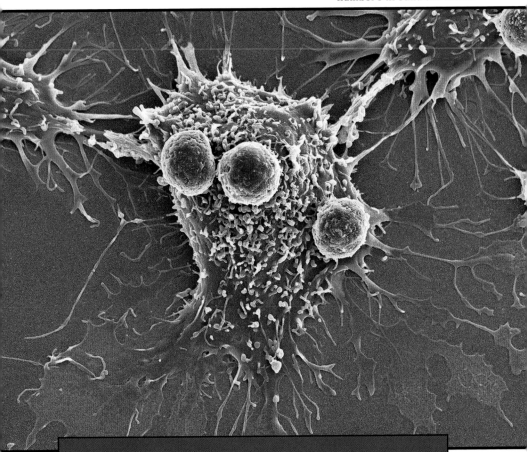

This colored scan shows (blue) T lymphocyte cells attaching to (red) cancer. T lymphocyte cells are part of the immune system and fight infection in the body.

infection or disease. Once the number of CD4 cells in a person's body falls below a certain amount, the person's HIV has reached the final stage, AIDS. One can also be diagnosed with AIDS if certain infections and cancers are contracted because HIV has made the immune system ineffective.

The National Institutes of Health (NIH) defines AIDS as "the most serious stage of HIV infection" that "results from the destruction of the infected person's immune system."

AIDS Defined

The Centers for Disease Control and Prevention (CDC) further explains the disease by defining each word in its name as follows:

- "Acquired" means that the disease is not hereditary, but develops after birth from contact with a disease-causing agent (in this case, HIV).
- "Immune deficiency" means that the disease is characterized by a weakening of the immune system.
- "Syndrome" refers to a group of symptoms that collectively indicate or characterize a disease. In the case of AIDS, this can include the development of certain infections or cancers, as well as a decrease in the number of certain cells in a person's immune system.

How It All Began

During the late 1970s and early 1980s, doctors became aware that an increasing number of people were suffering from several rare illnesses. One of these illnesses was a respiratory disease, Pneumocystis carinii pneumonia (PCP), which was usually a problem only for cancer patients undergoing chemotherapy. Another was a rare skin cancer, Kaposi's sarcoma, which, until then, mostly affected Mediterranean or Jewish men older than fifty years old who would usually live for years after diagnosis. However, the men becoming ill with these diseases were much younger and had previously been healthy. The diseases progressed so rapidly within their bodies that it appeared as if their immune systems were no longer working to resist them. Consequently, the men became weak and died. The number of cases recognized by doctors in cities across the United States grew from a few dozen in 1980 to several thousand within five years.

The First Victims

At first, very little was known about what was happening. Who was becoming ill? Was this a disease caused by a germ, or was it an immune system illness resulting from drug abuse? Would this condition spread among people at work or school or in cities?

Many of the first people diagnosed with this condition were homosexual men. Because of this, their condition was referred to as gay-related immunodeficiency, or GRID. However, the condition also showed up in intravenous drug users—male and female—who weren't homosexuals.

Another group of people affected were hemophiliacs. These people (almost all male) have a rare condition from birth that makes it hard for their blood to clot. They need to have regular injections of a clotting factor derived from blood donations. The wives of some infected hemophiliacs also became ill, and that alarmed the medical community even further.

It soon became clear that the illness was contagious, which means that someone could catch it from someone else. It was being passed from the sick men to their sexual partners, both male and female. Another clue came from the fact that intravenous drug abusers sometimes share needles, which can mean a drop of blood is passed from one person to another. It became obvious that the illness

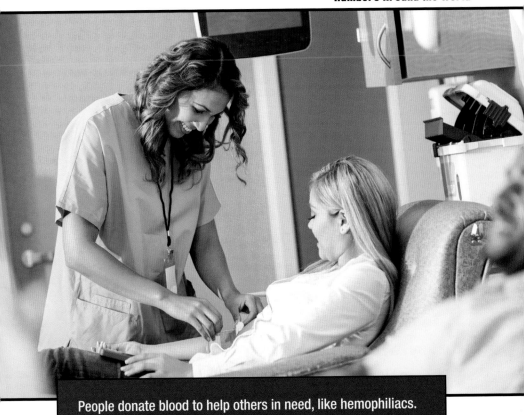

People donate blood to help others in need, like hemophiliacs. Those with the blood disorder need transfusions because their blood cannot clot on its own.

must be caused by something that could be carried in blood. Doctors checked among patients who had received blood transfusions or organ donations and found a few other people who were affected by this new disease.

The Culprit

Hospital and laboratory workers all around the world conducted research and found out what was happening: a previously unknown and rare virus was spreading from person to person. As people travel from place to place, some carry viruses inside their bodies unknowingly because they do not appear to be ill. Most of these viruses cause the common cold or other diseases that are treatable. But this disease was different. It was new.

The new disease made a person's immune system stop working so that the person would become ill from multiple causes and die. It was similar in some ways to the immune system weakness suffered by some people being treated for cancer. It was as if a person had acquired the very rare illness of being born with little or no immune system. In 1982, this disease was named acquired immune deficiency syndrome or acquired immunodeficiency syndrome (AIDS).

The Truth

In 1983, the Institut Pasteur in France recognized that a virus was the cause of AIDS. This virus was named human immunodeficiency virus (HIV). Researchers now understood that the virus moved from one person to another by the exchange of semen, blood, or vaginal secretions during sexual contact—or by coming into contact with the blood of an infected person, most likely through needle sharing and blood transfusions.

Another breakthrough was a test, created in 1985, that checked for HIV antibodies in a person's blood.

Scientists study DNA to try and discover where a disease comes from and how best to fight it. Researchers now know a lot about HIV and how to keep those with the virus healthy.

If a person has HIV, his or her immune system makes antibodies to try to kill the virus. Developing this test was crucial because a person with HIV might not look or feel ill for months or even years and may therefore unwittingly pass on the disease to others.

The Origin

HIV is a virus that used to be very rare and once affected only a few types of monkeys and chimpanzees in Africa. It is related to simian immunodeficiency virus, a similar immune deficiency virus that affects monkeys and apes (simians). People were exposed to HIV when they caught the monkeys for food or kept them as pets. Perhaps by being scratched or bitten, these people were exposed to the virus in the monkey's blood. There are a few human blood samples more than fifty years old that test positive for HIV.

A Global Epidemic

Though AIDS began as a rare infection in West Africa some fifty years ago, there are now people dying of the disease in every part of the world.

According to HIV.gov, a website run by US Department of Health and Human Services, more than 160,000 children fifteen years and younger were infected with HIV in 2016. Most of these children contracted the disease from their mothers during pregnancy, childbirth, or via breastfeeding. They live

A health care worker in South Africa helps a patient with her medication. It is very important to take the correct medicine for HIV, otherwise resistance to the virus can build up.

mainly live in sub-Saharan Africa. In fact, according to UNAIDS, 95 percent of new HIV infections occur in eastern Europe, central Asia, the Middle East, and North Africa. Eastern and southern Africa account for 16 percent of new infections. But many people are working to improve these numbers.

90-90-90

During the 20th International AIDS Conference in Melbourne, Australia, in 2014, a new initiative was announced to help fight the spread of HIV, called 90-90-90. It was based on the idea that by 2020:

- 90 percent: of people living with HIV know their status
- 90 percent: of people living with HIV who know their status are on treatment
- 90 percent: of people on treatment are virally suppressed

Viral suppression protects those who have HIV from developing further symptoms and greatly decreases the risk that they will transmit the disease to others. This campaign has had great success in eastern and southern Africa, the areas most affected by HIV, according to UNAIDS.

Michel Sidibé, UNAIDS executive director, wrote in the 2017 Global Update:

Families, communities, cities and countries have witnessed a transformation, with access to HIV treatment accelerating in the past three years. A record 19.5 million people are accessing antiretroviral therapy, and for the first time more than half of all people living with HIV are on treatment.

But there is still work to be done. "We live in fragile times, where gains can be easily reversed. The biggest challenge to moving forward is complacency," he reminded readers.

There is much work to be done to stop the spread of HIV, but there are many people working hard to end the spread of this disease.

CHAPTER TWO

Preventing the Spread of HIV

Because many of the first people to be diagnosed with AIDS were homosexual men, there were rumors at first that only gay men ever got this disease. This is not true. There are several ways one can get HIV, and once you learn about them, you will know how to keep yourself safe.

HIV and Sex

HIV can be spread through bodily fluids—blood, semen, and vaginal fluids—during vaginal or anal sexual contact. It can also be transmitted when bodily fluids come in contact with an open sore or cut.

Having protected sex is very important. It keeps you and your partner safe—and any future partners either of you might have. Think ahead and prepare.

If you are going to have sex, it is important to have protected sex. This means preventing contact with bodily fluids by using a condom. Unprotected sexual contact means that no barrier is used. Even if you're having sex for the first time, it's important to have protected sex. Even if both partners are HIV positive, they should still have protected sex to avoid being infected with different versions of HIV.

The sex of the people engaging in sexual contact does not matter. The virus can be transmitted from a man to a woman, from a woman to a man, from a man to a man, or from a woman to a woman. If a man who has HIV does not wear a condom, the virus in his semen and preseminal fluid could infect his partner. A woman who has HIV could infect her partner with the virus from her vaginal fluids. Any tiny cut or sore inside a vagina, anus, or mouth or on a penis would make it easy for the virus to pass into a person's body. A tiny sore might be too small to see or feel.

Oral Sex

The risk of contracting HIV through oral sex is low, according to the Centers for Disease Control and Prevention. Here are some ways to be safe while having oral sex:

- Keep the male partner from ejaculating in his partner's mouth
- Use a barrier like a condom or dental dam
- If a partner has HIV, he or she should be on medicine to treat the HIV

Safe-Sex Specifics

Abstinence, or not having sexual intercourse, is the only sure way to avoid contracting HIV by sexual contact. However, if you're going to have sex, then it is important to practice safe sex. Sexual touching does not have to be high-risk behavior. Kissing, touching with hands, and rubbing bodies will not transmit HIV from one person to another. Masturbating by yourself or with someone watching will not transmit HIV.

Intercourse is much less likely to transmit the virus if a barrier is used, such as a latex condom or dental dam. Avoid condoms that are made from animal membranes because germs can get through them. A lubricating cream or jelly should also be used, one that kills HIV and is spermicidal (kills sperm). This will make the barrier less likely to break, and if the barrier does break, the lubricant will be there to kill sperm or the virus. The lubricant should be a water-based brand. It is unsafe to use Vaseline, baby oil, and cooking oil as lubricants because these may cause the condom to break.

A woman can use a lubricant and a female condom to line her vagina if her male partner is not using a condom. If a woman is using the birth control pill, her male partner should still use a condom. The Pill offers no protection against sexually transmitted diseases.

If a woman is using a diaphragm, cervical cap, or sponge for birth control, even with lubricant, this is not enough protection for safe sex. These methods of birth control block sperm from entering a woman's uterus, but they would not block HIV.

A person who is allowing a penis, finger, or anything else to enter her or his anus should use lubricant in addition to a condom, as the anus is very easily damaged. Any tiny sores could allow HIV to enter the body.

A dental dam is a sheet of latex that can be used between a woman's vagina and a person's mouth or between an anus and a mouth. If you can't find dental dams at a store, you can make one by unrolling a condom and cutting it open along one side to make a flat sheet of latex. Although the lubricant may not taste very good, it is safe to get in the mouth during sex. Latex gloves are another option—a glove can be used to cover the fingers or a sex toy, and another glove can be cut open to make a flat sheet of latex for a dental dam.

Monogamy

Monogamy is when you have sex with only one person at a time, like in a marriage. One good reason to be in a committed relationship is that the fewer people you have sex with—and the fewer people your partner has sex with, the lower your chances are of getting a sexually transmitted disease, like HIV. Trust and honesty are very important in committed relationships.

Pregnancy, Childbirth, and Breastfeeding

The good news is that teen pregnancy has declined. Dr. Elise Berlan, a physician in adolescent medicine at Nationwide Children's Hospital, told CNN's Susan Scotti that this is in part because "data [from previous years] really suggests it is access to contraceptives and use of contraceptives that has really led to these kind of changes." She said, in particular, "most teens are using some form of birth control," the top method

Transmitting HIV from a pregnant mother to her baby has become much less common. If the pregnant woman stays on the proper medicine, the baby is likely to be safe.

being "the condom, followed by withdrawal and the Pill." But remember, withdrawing before ejaculation and taking birth control pills cannot prevent HIV. Even preseminal fluid, which comes out of a penis before ejaculation, can carry HIV.

HIV can be transmitted from a pregnant mother to her unborn child or through a nursing mother's milk for her baby. This is sometimes called vertical transmission. Fortunately, this has become less common. Especially if the pregnant woman begins taking medication for her HIV right away, the risk for transmission to the baby is much more unlikely.

Drug Use

The risk of spreading HIV through drug use by shared intravenous needles is very high. Injecting a needle into your arm can get blood on or in the needle. Then if someone else puts the same needle into his or her body, he or she can also be injecting your blood into himself or herself. And the virus can survive in a needle up to forty-two days, according to the CDC. Even cleaning a needle with bleach won't completely kill the virus.

Nearly one in ten new HIV cases are from injection drug use or injection drug use combined with male-to-male sexual contact. Drug use increases the likelihood of risky sexual behavior, including having unprotected sex, not taking HIV medicine and then having unprotected sex, and more, according to the CDC.

Other diseases such as viral hepatitis can be transmitted by sharing needles. Injecting drugs can also cause skin infections or abscesses, a swollen area of pus. You are also at risk from overdosing, which can be fatal.

If you are injecting drugs and want to stop, there is help for you. Ask a parent or trusted adult. If you cannot stop using drugs, it is important to never share needles or syringes and to never use them more than once. There are programs that help drug abusers by providing clean needles.

Ways to Say No

It can be difficult to say no to sex or drug use, but your decisions should be respected by your friends, significant other, and family. No one has the right to make you do anything sexually that you don't want to, especially anything that makes you feel uncomfortable or puts you at risk. No one has the right to insist you use illegal drugs.

How can you respond to pressure about sex or drugs? Here are some things you can say:

- "I care about you, but I don't want to have sex."
- "I'm not ready, and since this is my body, I'll tell you when I am ready."
- "I'm not ready right now. Let's make a plan for how we'll be safe when we do have sex."
- "I am very sure. You heard me say no, and I mean it."
- "I'm taking care of my body, and I don't want to harm it with drugs."
- "Drugs are illegal, and I will not break the law."
- "Let's go do something else."

You can probably think of more things to say that would work better for the people you know. Just frowning and walking away without saying anything can express your feelings pretty clearly, too.

If you are uncomfortable and do not want to have sex or do anything sexual, you have the right to say no. Your body, your decision. Anyone who questions this is not worth your time.

If you do decide to have sex, be smart about it. You can't tell whether your partner might have HIV. In many cases, he or she might not know either. As mentioned, unprotected sex is risky, so use latex condoms during any sexual activity—vaginal, anal, and oral sex.

Are Blood Transfusions Dangerous?

Hemophiliacs need regular injections of a blood-clotting product (made from the blood cells of others) all their lives. They get this from blood transfusions from donors. Consequently, they are more vulnerable to the risk of a blood-carried disease.

Most people might need only a single transfusion in their lifetimes because of surgery or an accident, and even then they will need only one unit of blood donated by one person. But hemophiliacs need a blood product made by pooling several blood donations and sorting out the clotting factor and other parts for many uses. If one blood donor is HIV positive, many hemophiliacs could be infected.

In 1984, when people were just learning about HIV, a thirteen-year-old boy named Ryan White, a hemophiliac, was diagnosed with AIDS after receiving a blood transfusion. Ryan and his mother, Jeanne White Ginder, did a great deal of advocacy work for people to understand how you

(continued on the next page)

Ryan White was a hemophiliac who contracted AIDS from a blood transfusion when he was thirteen. He became a spokesperson to help the public understand those living with the disease.

(continued from the previous page)

can and cannot get HIV. They fought for Ryan's right to attend school. He died in 1990, just before his high school graduation.

Today, hemophiliacs living in the United States, and others needing blood transfusions, have very little chance of contracting HIV. Since 1986, people who donate blood have been questioned carefully about whether they have done anything that puts them at risk of HIV infection. And every unit of blood is also tested for HIV antibodies.

HIV-Safe Behavior

For many years, people feared coming into contact with HIV-infected people because they didn't understand how the disease was transmitted. However, HIV transmission mainly takes place through a number of high-risk behaviors, namely unprotected sex and needle sharing.

The following are some situations that will not lead to an HIV infection:

- Touching a doorknob that has been touched by a person who is HIV positive
- Being friends with or working with a person who is HIV positive

- Touching a toilet seat that has been used by a person who is HIV positive
- Donating blood
- Swimming in a pool with a person who is HIV positive
- Sharing a drink with an HIV-positive person or even drinking from the same straw
- Insect bites

The HIV Vaccine

Scientists are working hard around the world to develop an HIV vaccine. A vaccine, or immunization, is a substance that teaches your body how to fight a disease. If you get the vaccine when you are healthy, you will be able to fight it off when exposed. Though there is not an HIV vaccine yet, many hope there will be one available one day.

Myths & FACTS

Myth: You can get HIV from a tattoo.

Fact: According to the CDC, there are no known cases of someone getting HIV from a tattoo needle or piercing. But it's still important to be careful. If you want a tattoo or piercing, be sure to go to a licensed professional. Make sure that that professional uses new or sterilized needles, ink, and other materials.

Myth: You can get HIV from a kiss.

Fact: Open-mouth kissing an HIV-positive person results in infection very rarely, only if both partners have sores or bleeding gums. There is no evidence that the virus is ever spread through saliva, in fact saliva contains substances that stop HIV from being infectious. Closed-mouth kissing (dry kissing or social kissing) with an infected person is considered safe.

Myth: Any kind of birth control will protect against HIV.

Fact: You must use a barrier, like a condom, to keep from exchanging sperm or vaginal fluids with your partner. Birth control pills or spermicide is not enough protection.

CHAPTER THREE

HIV and the Body

HIV is a virus that attacks the immune system. But what exactly happens to the body when it is infected?

The HIV Retrovirus

Like other viruses, HIV cannot grow or reproduce on its own. A virus must infect the cells of a living organism—a person, an animal, or a plant—in order to make new copies of itself.

HIV is one of a special class of virus called retroviruses. A retrovirus uses a reverse version of some standard enzymes in our cells. Almost all organisms, including most viruses, store their genetic material on long molecules of DNA

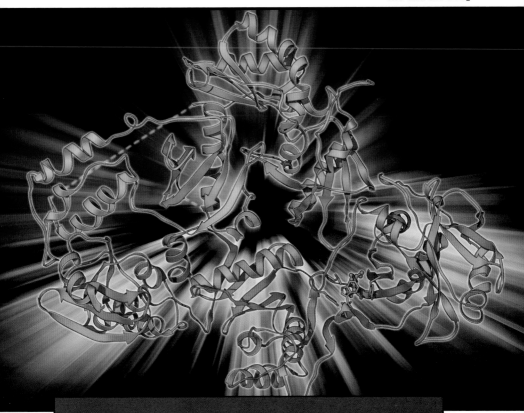

A molecular model of the HIV reverse transcription enzyme. The virus is able to integrate with human DNA. Researchers now understand much about the disease and how to slow it.

(deoxyribonucleic acid). But the genes of retroviruses are made of RNA (ribonucleic acid).

HIV has just nine genes. That's not many compared to the more than five hundred genes in some bacteria or around twenty thousand to twenty-five thousand genes in a human. However, these genes can mutate, making tiny changes in the virus.

Infiltrating the Body's Cells

When a virus gets inside a living cell, it uses the cell's copying process to make copies of itself. When this copying process is hijacked by a lethal virus such as HIV, the result is many copies of the virus and a dead cell.

HIV uses chemicals called enzymes to get into a cell, hide itself there, and get copies of itself made. Once inside a human cell, HIV uses an enzyme, reverse transcriptase, to convert its own viral RNA into DNA. In the cell's nucleus, this DNA is spliced into the human DNA by another HIV enzyme, called integrate. That integrated HIV DNA may remain dormant within a cell for a long time.

But when the cell becomes activated to make new proteins for many uses, it treats the HIV genes much like human genes. First, the cell uses human enzymes to convert the genes into messenger RNA, then the RNA is transported outside the nucleus to be a blueprint for producing new proteins and enzymes. Some of these RNA strands are complete copies of HIV, which are released from the cell in particles ready to infect other cells. Unlike most bacteria, HIV particles are too small to be seen with an ordinary microscope.

This process may seem very complicated. The most practical thing to know is that the enzymes used to convert or copy the virus can be slowed down, or inhibited, by certain drugs prescribed by doctors.

Signs of HIV

A person who is HIV positive can live for years without developing any symptoms. But there are some common warning signs of HIV infection. If you suffer from one of these common warning signs, do not be alarmed. It does not mean that you have HIV. Many other illnesses have similar symptoms. The symptoms of HIV infection are not unique, they just show that a person's immune system is being stressed. It's up to a doctor to diagnose the illness that is causing the symptoms. All you have to do is ask for an HIV test. It might be scary, but you can do it.

Here are some early signs of HIV infection, which may appear two to four weeks after infection, though not everyone who contracts the virus feels sick during this time:

- Swollen lymph nodes, flulike illness (usually experienced within weeks after exposure to HIV)
- Frequent fevers

Seeing a doctor when one thinks one has contracted HIV can be scary, but it is important. The sooner one gets on antiretroviral drugs to battle the virus, the better.

- Excessive sweating
- Unexplained fatigue
- Rapid weight loss
- Pneumonia
- Breathing difficulties
- Diarrhea that lasts longer than a week
- White spots or sores in the mouth and throat
- Blotches on or under the skin that are colored red, pink, purple, or brown

What Is a Lymph Node?

Lymph nodes are part of the immune system. They are small, bean-shaped organs that are also called glands. You can sometimes feel them in your neck, armpits, and groin. Other nodes are deep inside the body. Lymph nodes store immune cells, which can trap and destroy bacteria and viruses that enter the body. A lymph node swells as the immune cells inside the node attack foreign invaders.

HIV and AIDS Progression

The CDC recognizes several steps in the progression from HIV infection to AIDS. They are:

- **Acute infection:** The earliest stage, right after one is infected. Within two to four weeks, one might feel flulike symptoms for a week or so. This is because the body is executing its natural response to infection. During the acute infection stage, the newly infected person has a great deal of the virus in his or her blood and is very contagious.
- **Clinical latency:** This stage can also be called asymptomatic HIV infection or chronic HIV infection. HIV is still present in the body but reproduces at very low levels. How long this stage lasts depends on the person. If an HIV-infected person takes his or her medicine, this stage can be several decades long.
- **AIDS:** AIDS is diagnosed when you have a variety of symptoms, infections, and specific test results. The immune system is greatly damaged, and the infected person can get a

series of severe illnesses. Those with AIDS have a great amount of the virus in their system and are very contagious.

AIDS-Defining Illnesses

People whose infections have progressed to AIDS may be recognized by the diseases from which they are suffering. Because their immune systems are no longer working, people with AIDS are vulnerable to close to twenty illnesses, called AIDS-defining conditions. If an HIV-positive person contracts one of these diseases, his or her HIV has moved to the final stage, AIDS. Here are a few AIDS-defining illnesses:

- **Toxoplasmosis of the brain:** Lesions on the brain cause headaches, confusion, seizures, and blurred vision.
- **Wasting syndrome due to HIV:** Losing at least 10 percent of one's body weight due to diarrhea or a fever lasting at least thirty days.
- **Kaposi's sarcoma (KS):** A cancer that grows on the lining of lymph nodes or blood

vessels and can cause tumors on the skin or inside the mouth. Kaposi's sarcoma causes purplish marks called lesions on the skin, the linings of the digestive tract, and the lungs. KS was rare before the 1980s, but now most cases of KS occur in people with AIDS.

- **Invasive cervical cancer:** Cancer that has spread from the surface of the cervix deeper into the cervix or to other parts of the body. Women who are HIV positive have an increased risk of developing cervical cancer. There are no symptoms associated with the early stages of this cancer, but there is a test for the early cell changes, called a Pap test.
- **Recurrent pneumonia:** Persistent lung infection.
- **Lymphoma:** Cancer of the white blood cells (lymphocytes).

People who have AIDS are at a higher risk of suffering from certain mental disorders. Memory loss is one disorder, and another is dementia, a severe loss of mental capacity. Another common brain disorder, HIV neuropathy, causes many AIDS patients to lose feeling in their arms and legs.

It is important to note that many people suffer from these conditions without having AIDS. To be diagnosed with AIDS, a person must first be infected with HIV. Doctors carefully observe and count the

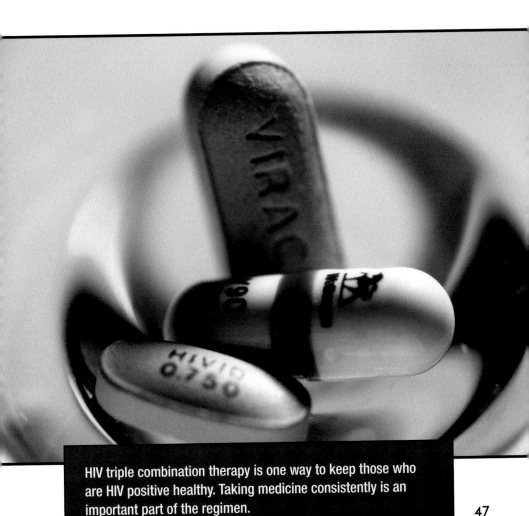

HIV triple combination therapy is one way to keep those who are HIV positive healthy. Taking medicine consistently is an important part of the regimen.

white blood cells of HIV patients. There are normally tens of thousands of white blood cells in a healthy body. When the T-helper cell count (also referred to as the CD4 count) drops below two hundred, a person is formally diagnosed with AIDS. One may also be diagnosed even if the HIV-positive patient's CD4 count is more than two hundred, if he or she has one or more of the AIDS-defining conditions.

Hope Ahead

Hearing the specifics of HIV and AIDS can be scary. But there is good news, we promise. According to AVERT, a United Kingdom–based organization that has been fighting HIV for thirty years, people with HIV are living longer—as long as they get treated. People living in the United States and Europe who have HIV but take the correct medications as prescribed can expect to live a normal lifetime. This means that if one contracted HIV at twenty years old and stayed on treatment, one could live to be seventy-eight. This is amazing news!

However, for those living in lower-income countries, the news is not as good. For example, someone with HIV in South Africa, which has the largest population of those living with the virus, could live a long life. But that is assuming he or she can overcome significant hurdles: including getting tested, accessing sometimes expensive medical treatment, and staying on that treatment.

Many organizations around the world, including UNAIDS, are working to bring treatment to everyone who needs it. But there is still work to be done.

CHAPTER FOUR

Getting Tested and Dealing with a Diagnosis

So you think you might have HIV. Or you're just concerned. Getting tested is easy—and even, in some places, free and anonymous.

Getting Tested

Everyone should know his or her HIV status, especially those who engage in or have engaged in any high-risk behavior. There's no need to wonder or worry if you might be HIV positive—get tested and you'll know for sure. The test for HIV is very reliable.

According to the CDC, there are 1.1 million people living in the United States with HIV. One in seven of those people do not know they have

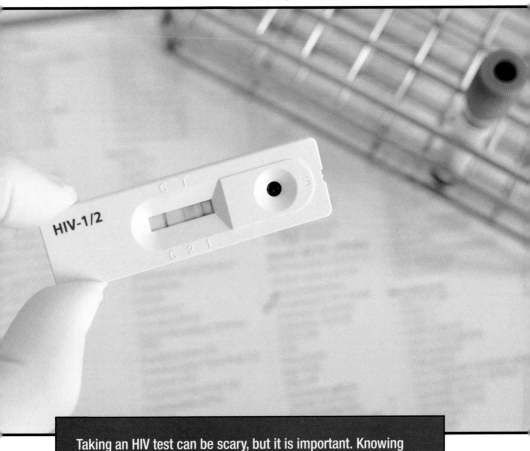

Taking an HIV test can be scary, but it is important. Knowing your status means keeping yourself—and any sexual partners you may have—safe.

it. Those people are at risk of transmitting HIV to others. Research also shows that most people who know that they are infected take steps to reduce their risk of infecting others. Given these two realities, it makes sense that increasing the number of people who know their HIV status can help to reduce HIV transmission. More importantly, more HIV-positive individuals would get the treatment they need. And the sooner an infected person gets treatment for HIV, the longer his or her life will be.

If you take an anonymous HIV test, you do not have to give your name. A unique code will be used to identify you instead. The only person who will know your actual test results is you. This type of test is available in most states.

Where to Get the Test

If you suspect you have HIV or AIDS, it is incredibly important to get tested. Don't be scared, take control. Remember, knowledge is power.

When you are ready to get tested, there are several places you can go:

- Doctor's office
- Clinic
- Mobile testing van
- Home HIV test

There are many websites that can help you find a testing place. Check gettested.cdc.gov to find somewhere near you.

The Tests

There are several types of HIV tests available, and which one you should take depends on the time period you were potentially exposed to the virus. Remember when you last had unprotected sex or shared a needle. This is an important date to keep in mind as it can help your doctor decide which type of test is best for you.

Rapid test: A health care provider will take your blood or oral fluid to test for HIV antibodies. Antibodies generally appear in an infected person's blood three to twelve weeks after exposure. You can wait for the results at the appointment. If your test is positive, you will need to have a follow-up test. This will tell you if you really have HIV or not.

Combination or fourth-generation test: This test looks for antigens and antibodies. Antigens are in the body during the acute infection stage, very early on. These tests can therefore detect infection sooner, two to six weeks from time of infection.

These tests are sent to a laboratory, so you will have to return for the results.

Nucleic acid test: This test looks for HIV itself in the blood. It is very expensive and not usually used unless the person was recently exposed to the virus and is showing early symptoms. This text can detect HIV one week after exposure.

If you get tested—great job! Just remember that you are only HIV negative so long as you avoid having unprotected sex and sharing needles. And,

National Testing Day

Because of the importance of knowing your HIV status, for your health and the health of those around you, the Centers for Disease Control and Prevention started National Testing Day. Begun in 1995, every June 27, people around the country are encouraged to get tested, empowering themselves through knowledge. Ignoring HIV will not make it go away. It will only make you sick.

as the website HIV.gov says, "If you get an HIV test within three months after a potential HIV exposure and the result is negative, get tested again in three more months to be sure."

The Test Itself Has No Risks

Are you hesitating to get your blood tested because you're worried that the needle used could possibly infect you? Or maybe you're hesitating about donating blood. You do not have to worry about this at all. There is no risk at all of contracting HIV or AIDS from having your blood tested or from donating blood. In Canada and the United States, all doctors, nurses, and blood technicians always use a brand-new, sterile needle for each person. No needles are ever reused on someone else. No one else's blood will ever be put into your body when a sample of your blood is taken or when you donate blood. You can have complete confidence.

The Ins and Outs of Home Testing

You can also use an at-home HIV test, if you would like. This test can be ordered online or bought in some drugstores. Make sure the test is FDA approved. This will help to ensure that it is safe to use and accurate.

Here are two types of at-home tests available now:

Home Access HIV-1 Test System: With this test, you prick your finger, then send the sample to a licensed laboratory. Your results can sometimes be available the next day. If the test is positive, you can have a follow-up test right away.

OraQuick In-Home HIV Test: You can do this test at home by swabbing your mouth for an oral sample. Your results will be available in twenty minutes. If your results come back positive, you need a follow-up test. There are two caveats to using this test: because HIV antibodies take longer to appear in saliva, this test will only find HIV that

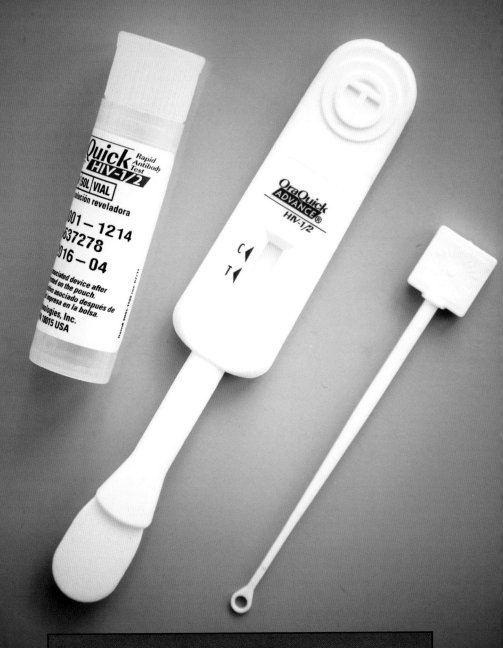

At-home HIV tests allow even more people to find out their HIV status. Remember to read the directions carefully, and follow up with a doctor if there are questions or concerns.

has been living in the body for a longer period of time. Also, this test reports false positives for one of every twelve tests. This means you may get a positive diagnosis but not really have HIV. This is why getting a follow-up test is so important.

Notwithstanding the convenience of the home tests, most HIV experts would advise people to have their HIV tests done in a medical setting, where counseling (both before and after the test) is a part of the testing process. Most people dread the thought of being HIV positive and are therefore extremely anxious about taking the test. Counseling helps to alleviate these anxieties, particularly if the result comes back positive.

Dealing with an HIV-Positive Diagnosis

For most people, learning that you are HIV positive may be the most devastating news that you can receive. However, it is important to realize that nowadays, HIV is not a death sentence. Many people, like basketball great Magic Johnson, go on to live long, productive lives after they discover their HIV-positive status. You can, too.

A positive HIV test doesn't mean you have AIDS. However, HIV can progress to AIDS if it remains untreated. Therefore, some of the first things you should do after learning your status is to find out more about the disease, seek support, and see an HIV doctor. Chances are that if you did your HIV test in a medical setting, the doctor, nurse, or a counselor there would have given you some information about how to go about doing these things.

Telling a Loved One

Many people recall feeling terribly alone when they first tested positive for HIV. Although this is a normal reaction, it is important to recognize that there is an incredible network of support organizations across the United States eager to offer aid, information, and comfort to HIV-positive individuals. However, no matter how willing these groups are to help, they recognize the

Finding out one is HIV positive can be a terrifying experience. Now is the time to reach out to a loved one. There are so many ways to still live a healthy life.

importance of being able to share your diagnosis with someone you trust, especially if that person is a loved one.

Ideally, teenagers who test positive for HIV without their parents' knowledge should inform their parents right away. No matter how disappointed or upset you think your parents may become, it is generally unwise to keep such a critical diagnosis from the very people who are most responsible for your well-being.

Enlist the help of someone else, like a counselor from the clinic where you did the test, to break the news to your parents if you feel you cannot face them alone. Hopefully, your parents will support you no matter how shocked they are by the news. If, however, your parents are not supportive, choose someone else who you think will be able to handle the news and keep your secret. Although it is difficult to tell how people will respond, you should have an idea of who will be there for you.

Regardless of the support you get from your family, you should consider joining a support group for people who were recently diagnosed with HIV. (There are support groups for parents of HIV-positive people, too.) Such groups can be instrumental for easing your anxieties, providing you with reliable information, and steering you in the right direction for the various services, including medical treatment, that you might need.

Doctors and Doses

If you receive an HIV diagnosis, it is important to see to a doctor. You might need some time to absorb the information, so consider doing some research yourself. Use some of the resources listed at the back of this book. Try to read only reputable sources that will tell you the truth. Then, it's time to make a doctor's appointment.

Finding a Doctor

The initial test determines only your HIV status; so you'll need to undergo further tests to find out how the virus is affecting your body and how soon you'll need treatment. HIV care is ongoing.

Finding a doctor does not need to be difficult. Your current primary care doctor may be an HIV specialist, or he or she may be able to refer you to one. You may also seek the advice of other HIV-positive people, a support group, AIDS services organizations, or even the clinic or medical center where you did the test.

Some people interview several doctors before signing on as a patient. However you go about selecting your HIV specialist, here are a few questions you should keep in mind in deciding who is right for you:

- Does the doctor have experience dealing with HIV?
- Does the doctor make you feel comfortable?
- Did the doctor answer your questions clearly?
- Is the doctor available enough?
- Does he or she address your whole health and not just your HIV status?

Your First Doctor Visit

Your first visit to the HIV specialist you've selected to oversee your care is a very important one. First, you'll be establishing a new relationship with someone with whom you'll be working to make informed decisions

It is important to find a doctor who listens and understands. Having HIV is a lifelong journey. Select someone whom you are comfortable talking with.

about your treatment. It's likely that you'll be very anxious, and the doctor probably will anticipate this and try to reassure you that despite your diagnosis, you can lead a healthy and productive life. This is a good time for you to ask questions, so you may want to jot some down beforehand and take them with you to the appointment.

In addition to asking you questions about your medical history, the doctor will do a physical examination and order blood tests. These blood tests will help your doctor determine how the virus is affecting your body. The two standard tests include a CD4 count and a viral load test. The CD4 count reports the number of CD4 cells (or T cells) in a sample of your blood. CD4 cells are the white blood cells that fight infection but are targeted by the HIV virus. Therefore, the higher the count, the better the result. The viral load test measures the amount of HIV in a sample of your blood. It shows how well your immune system is controlling the virus. The lower the load, the better the result. Together, the CD4 count and the viral load count provide a baseline (or initial) measurement for future tests.

Your doctor is also likely to order drug resistance tests, which determine whether your HIV has developed resistance to any HIV medication. You may wonder how your virus could be resistant to HIV medications before you've even taken them. The answer is that drug resistance is transmitted along with the virus. In other words, you will inherit whatever drug resistance the person who infected you with HIV has. Your doctor may also do other tests, including:

- A complete blood count (CBC), which checks all the different types of blood cells.
- A blood chemistry profile, which shows how well your liver and kidney are working and measures the lipids (fats) and sugar (glucose) in your blood.
- Tests for other sexually transmitted diseases (STDs).
- Tests for other infections, like hepatitis, tuberculosis, or toxoplasmosis.
- If you're female, your doctor is also likely to order a pregnancy test and a Pap smear.

Antiretroviral Therapy

Talk with your doctor about when to start antiretroviral therapy, or ART. It is especially urgent to begin right away if you:

- Are pregnant

- Have HIV that has progressed to AIDS
- Have certain HIV-related infections
- Are very recently infected with HIV

Talk with your doctor about the pros and cons of ART. It is very important that you follow the directions for your medicine very closely. If you have a schedule that makes it difficult to take medicine at the same time every day, or if you are worried about being able to afford the pills, tell your doctor so that together, you can plan. Remember that by sticking to your regimen, you will keep your HIV in check—and lower the chances of infecting others.

Getting Care if You Can't Afford It

Health care is expensive, but there are options available for you if you are HIV positive and do not have the money to go to the doctor. First, talk with your parent, if you can, or a trusted adult. He or she can help you find resources. Here are a few options you can look into:

- **The Ryan White & Global HIV/AIDS Program:** This program provides services to half a million people in need each year, including access to HIV medical care and medicine. There are restrictions on who can be helped by this program, see their website for more information, listed at the end of this book.
- **The Affordable Care Act and Medicaid:** This plan allows you to buy health insurance if you

(continued on the next page)

A doctor will ask a lot of questions and take blood samples at your first visit. This helps determine how far the virus has progressed. Be honest and try not to be too scared.

(continued from the previous page)

or your family does not have any. There are also specific resources to help you find out if you qualify for Medicaid, a federal program that helps those who cannot afford health care on their own.

Staying on Schedule with ART

Here are some tips to remember to take your medicine at the same time, every day:

- Get a seven-day pillbox and lay out your pills each week.
- Set an alarm on your phone so you make sure to take your medicine at the same time every day.
- Plan ahead if you will be traveling.
- Ask a parent or friend to check in or remind you about taking your medicine.

Possible Prescriptions

ART is used to control the reproduction of the virus, thereby slowing the progression of HIV-related disease. To date, the US Food and Drug

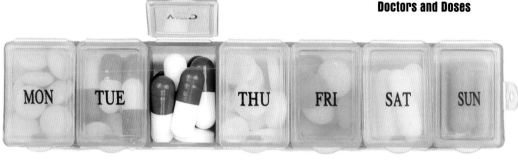

Being vigilant about taking ART at the correct time is an important part of staying healthy. Work out ways to remember your medicine—it's important!

Administration (FDA) has approved nine categories of antivirals, which work against HIV in different ways. The nine categories of antiretrovirals are:

- **Nonnucleoside reverse transcriptase inhibitors (NNRTIs):** These drugs interrupt the first step HIV takes to copy itself by binding to and disabling reverse transcriptase, a protein necessary to the copying process
- **Nucleoside reverse transcriptase inhibitors (NRTIs):** Like the NNRTIs, NRTIs also interrupt the first step HIV takes to make copies.
- **Protease inhibitors (PIs):** These drugs interrupt the last stage HIV takes to copy itself by disabling protease, a protein necessary for the copying process.

- **Fusion inhibitors:** These drugs work by blocking HIV from entering CD4 cells.
- **CCR5 antagonists:** These drugs block HIV from entering cells.
- **Integrase inhibitors:** These drugs block an enzyme HIV needs.
- **Post-attachment inhibitors:** These drugs block CD4 receptors to keep HIV out.
- **Pharmacokinetic enhancers:** These drugs increase how well HIV medicine works.

Most patients take a combination of drugs from different classes. This is called combination therapy.

Choosing a Regimen

All those medicine types may be confusing to you, which is why it is important to talk with your doctor. When you choose a regimen, here are some things you, your doctor, and your parents or loved ones should consider:

- Other diseases

- Possible side effects
- Cost
- Convenience

The goal of ART is to keep your viral load low so that HIV does not begin to make you sick. With a low viral load, you are also less likely to infect someone else, though you still need to take precautions, like never having unprotected sex and never sharing needles. Once you start taking your regimen, it should take three to six months for your viral load to become undetectable. You will still have HIV, but you can live a happy, full life.

Be honest with your doctor and family about how you are feeling and concerns that you might have. Together, you can make a plan that will work and keep you healthy.

Other Medicines

Depending on your other health concerns, your doctor may prescribe medication that is not directly related to your HIV status. For example, antibiotics can be helpful to cure diseases that strike when a person's immune system is not working well. Opportunistic infections take advantage of the lack of resistance in HIV patients and are no longer small health problems. Some of these opportunistic infections are merely uncomfortable, like thrush, an infection of *Candida* yeast in the mouth. Others can be fatal if untreated. Often it is an opportunistic infection that kills a person with AIDS. Even vitamin pills can help a person with HIV remain as well as possible for as long as possible. Vitamins and antibiotics are surprisingly helpful treatments for people who did not have good health before becoming infected with HIV. Talk it over with your doctor before taking anything, but be honest about how you're feeling. Your doctor should be there to help you.

Follow-Up Visits

After you begin taking antiretroviral medications, you will be required to visit your doctor every three or four months so that he or she can monitor how well your treatment is working. During these visits, your doctor will order a CD4 count and a viral load test to measure against the baseline measurements from your first visit. He or she will also monitor your general health.

You should use these scheduled visits to further develop your relationship with your doctor. When he or she asks you how things are going, be

Keeping track of medicine, doctor visits, and more can be difficult. Using a digital calendar or a paper planner can help everything stay organized.

prepared to give him or her a full account of your health over the last few months. Consider making a list of the questions and issues you want to raise with your doctor. It may help you to keep a diary, noting the following:

- Missed doses
- New or changed symptoms that you've experienced since your last visit
- Major changes in your life that may affect your level of stress
- Your lab results (CD4, viral load, etc.)
- Other medications, vitamins, or nutritional supplements that you're taking

10 Great Questions to Ask Your Doctor About HIV

1. What are the risks and benefits of HIV treatment?

2. What other diseases am I at risk for?

3. How can I avoid transmitting HIV to others?

4. How can I achieve and maintain a healthier lifestyle?

5. What should I do if I miss a dose of my HIV medication?

6. What should I do if I have problems sticking to my treatment regimen?

7. Can I infect someone else if my viral load is undetectable?

8. What are the likely side effects of the medications I take? Which side effects are serious?

9. Will the side effects go away by themselves? Are there any side effects that should prompt me to stop taking my medication?

10. How do I know if the drugs aren't working anymore?

CHAPTER SIX

Life with a Positive Diagnosis

So you got tested and found out your status as an HIV-positive person. You went to the doctor and are taking your medicine on time, as prescribed. What now?

Life with HIV

HIV likely will factor into your everyday schedule in many ways, especially after you begin treatment, but it doesn't need to dominate your life. The sooner you get used to your new routine, the better you'll be able to enjoy the rest of your time. There are many things you can do to maintain or improve your quality of life. Perhaps the most important ones are making sure that you stay healthy, develop a good support system, pursue your dreams, and leave room for fun.

There is life after an HIV-positive diagnosis. So many others have learned to live with the disease, and you can, too. With the help of a good doctor, family, and friends, life will go on.

How to Feel Good

Of course, it is crucial that you follow your doctor's advice and keep your medical appointments. If you are taking prescription drugs, you must be careful to take every dose, as missed doses make the drugs less effective. However, there's more to being healthy than simply taking your meds.

Feed and Move Your Body

Eating well and exercising are essential for HIV-positive individuals, whose immune systems are constantly under assault by the virus. Try eating a wide variety of fruits and vegetables of different colors. This will ensure that you are getting an array of vitamins in your diet.

Try to get at least thirty minutes of moderate to vigorous physical activity every day. Examples of moderate exercise include walking briskly, dancing, and bicycling. Vigorous exercise includes running, swimming, and basketball.

Nutritionist Alan Lee says that vitamins and minerals offer many benefits to people living with HIV, such as boosting your immune system and overall health. His list of foods loaded with vitamins and minerals includes butternut squash, yams, watermelon, fish, whole-grain cereal, sweet potatoes, peaches, oatmeal, 1 percent milk, collard greens, whole-wheat pasta, kale, pumpkin, oranges, wild rice, and chicken. You can also use basic vitamin and mineral supplements to increase those benefits.

Here's Lee's guide to buying and using supplements:

- Look for a complete list of nutrients on the label that supplies 100 percent of the daily value.
- Look for "USP," "NSF," or "Consumer Lab" on the label to make sure you're getting what the label actually states. These are organizations

Eating well is especially important when one has HIV. Filling a dinner plate with vegetables of all different colors is a great way to stay healthy.

that watch over vitamin production.

- Always take your vitamins with food.
- Take your vitamins with your HIV medications, unless your medications require that you take them on an empty stomach.
- Discuss your vitamin and mineral supplementation plan with your doctor to make sure that your supplements don't interact with your medications.

Avoid Risky Behaviors

Of course, good general health includes avoiding risky behavior. Being HIV positive doesn't give you a free pass to continue or start sharing needles during drug use or having unprotected sex. On the contrary, having HIV is a strong reason not to engage in these behaviors. In addition to exposing others to infection, you run the risk of superinfection, which is becoming infected with another strain of HIV. Superinfection increases the likelihood of your developing resistance to anti-HIV medication, which will reduce the treatment options available to you.

In addition, a person's immune system may be weakened by drug abuse. This can make it easier to become ill with many kinds of diseases, including AIDS. Drug abuse can also interfere with the medicines prescribed by a doctor. It's important to be honest with your doctor about any substance use, whether it's a lot or a little, and whether it's alcohol, illegal drugs, misused prescription drugs, or marijuana. Even cigarettes and other tobacco products, though legal, are addictive and have profound health effects. If you are abusing intravenous drugs or any substance, consider seeking help.

Identify Yourself

People living with HIV should consider wearing a MedicAlert bracelet or necklace, which comes with a unique ID number that allows first responders and health professionals to retrieve your health records and personal information through the service. Many people wear them for many health reasons. Any doctor's office or clinic, and even

(continued on the next page)

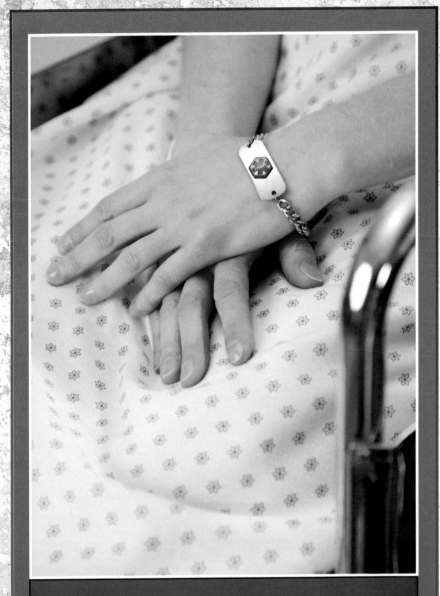

A medical alert bracelet can let medical professionals know in an emergency that you are HIV positive. This can help to keep you and those around you safe.

(continued from the previous page)

most drugstores, will have information on how to register for a MedicAlert tag.

In case of an accident, emergency workers always look to see if a person is wearing a MedicAlert tag. The tag can be something you show to one person in a crowded room, for example, if you need to tell a nurse you are HIV positive but don't feel like saying it out loud for everyone in the waiting room to hear.

If someone peeks at your MedicAlert tag and asks why you are wearing it, you have a choice. You can tell them the reason, let them read it, or quietly say that it's private.

Keeping Others Healthy

If you are HIV positive, you have a responsibility not to infect other people with the virus. Be honest about your HIV status. People who care about you deserve to know. It's hard to risk rejection, but being honest is being responsible.

- Tell previous and current sexual partners that you are HIV positive.

- If you hope to have a new sexual partner, tell this person you are HIV positive before becoming intimate.
- Do not have unprotected sex, even if you previously had unprotected sex with this person.
- Do not share your razor or toothbrush with anyone.
- If you become pregnant, or if you are thinking about having a child, talk to your doctor right away.
- If you abuse drugs, do not share needles. More importantly, get help for your addiction.

Disclosing Your HIV Status

Being HIV positive isn't something that will be obvious to everyone. Even having AIDS is not as visible as losing an arm or using a wheelchair. It is a health difference that doesn't show, and it's up to you to decide what difference it makes in the ways you behave with the people you meet.

It's not your job to educate everybody you see about AIDS and HIV. But it doesn't hurt to think ahead once in a while. What would you say if someone asked you a question? How could you help a stranger who had an accident? When is it best to be anonymous?

Some days you will make different decisions about what to say and what actions to take. But you can always use your knowledge about HIV and AIDS to help you be confident that you are making good decisions for your health and for your community.

Does Everyone Know?

If you live in a large city, probably no one at all will know if you are HIV positive, unless you have told them yourself. Don't be self-conscious about how you look or whether anyone can tell. Don't waste a lot of time wondering if strangers are looking at you or thinking about you. Just go about your activities as you normally do. Nobody can tell just from looking at you.

If you live in a small town or very connected neighborhood, someone you meet casually might know that you are HIV positive because you and your family may have told that person. If you don't know how you feel about that, remember that you probably know something about many other people as well.

Some people who are HIV positive or have AIDS find it easier to share the news with a group (perhaps at church, school, or a community center), rather than to try to keep it a secret. This sharing can be a way to be confident in the company of your neighbors. It can also be a way to learn who is afraid of the disease or ignorant. Perhaps your group will ask a health center to hold an information session for the community. However, you should always be aware that by disclosing your status, you risk rejection.

Emotional Health

When people need health care, they also need emotional and spiritual care. There are many kinds of support available. Having emotional and spiritual support can not only make you feel better in your mind, it can help your physical health as well.

Religious Guidance and More

Some people get the support they need from religious faith, others from psychology and scientific disciplines. You may want to consider traditional supports already in use by your family and culture. Maybe you want to go to a religious service. Perhaps you would like to see a therapist. Maybe your school counselor is easy to talk to. There are many resources available to help you as you deal with the emotional upheaval of dealing with HIV. There are libraries and resource centers to consult, and you may get good recommendations from your friends and health care providers. If you have a good emotional and spiritual adviser, that person will work to help you live well. The hardest part can just be asking, but you are worth the effort.

Support Groups

There are support groups for people living with AIDS and HIV. Support groups can bring you a great deal of comfort since you will meet people who share similar emotions and experiences. Just knowing that other people are facing the same challenges can help you feel less isolated or lonely.

The people in a support group are people like yourself, whose lives are affected by HIV and AIDS. They can help you understand treatment methods and ways to adjust your lifestyle. Usually one of them will have some training as a facilitator and will be able to help find resources or the answers to questions..

Talking with a therapist can be a great idea if you or someone in your family has been diagnosed with HIV. Someone outside the situation can provide insight and help.

It can make you feel isolated and alone if you are HIV positive and have not told your family or friends. If you're scared of what they will say or you're just not ready to share yet, that's understandable. A support group can help you prepare yourself for how you will tell your friends and family.

You can be affected by AIDS, even if you are not the person infected with HIV. Finding out that someone you care about is HIV positive is very upsetting. Support groups help friends and family as well, not only the person who is HIV positive.

When More Help Is Needed

While there have been great strides in helping those with HIV stay healthy, there are times when HIV does turn into AIDS. And that is when you and your family might need additional support.

Physical Care

A person who is HIV positive but at an asymptomatic stage may not need much physical help at all.

However, someone whose disease has progressed may need assistance for daily living. On occasion, the care of a trained nurse may be needed, but friends or family can often learn how to care for the majority of a person's physical needs.

By the time a person is diagnosed with AIDS, there will be good days and bad days, but the person is likely to need physical care much of the time. Family members and friends can take turns helping where needed. Or perhaps one helper will concentrate on one aspect, like running errands and doing laundry, while another will look after nursing care.

The changes in what a person is physically able to do can be very upsetting for everyone. It can also be an opportunity to recognize that we all live in real bodies, bodies that change with time and health and chance. There will certainly be emotional reactions as well.

When a Hospice Is the Answer

People living with AIDS often rely on hospice organizations. A hospice can be a palliative care (specialized medical care for those with a serious illness) hospital, where people go for nursing care when they are dying. The hospice organization can also be for people who want to be in control of their lives as they confront their terminal illnesses.

In a hospice program, the doctors, registered nurses, counselors, and social workers work with a patient and his or her own doctor to manage pain and plan treatments. They provide advice and support. Most of their services are offered at the patient's home.

Helping Others

Sometimes looking outside yourself and your own circumstances can help you to feel better and to learn and grow. There is much you can do to improve the world.

What Difference Can I Make?

You are only one person. But each day, you can do something positive to make that day better. Even small improvements are real and can be special.

You have the ability to be nice to the people who live in your home. A kind word, helping someone with homework or housework, telling a funny story, or listening to someone else's news: these are all things that show that you care. They can be done even by a person who usually needs the most help from others.

You can also think bigger. Many teens today are involved in activism for causes that are important to them. You can volunteer for a political campaign. You can support a cause that is important to you by attending protests or writing postcards. You have the power to change the world, and having HIV does not change that.

Being an Example

Some things about AIDS and HIV are private. But there are also times when it is proper to speak in public about HIV/AIDS, to go to a meeting, or to march in a parade. A loop of red ribbon pinned on a shirt or jacket is a visible reminder that you care.

There are activities you can do with other people in your community to show support for people with HIV or AIDS. There are educational programs. Some communities have fundraising events to raise money for a local clinic or hospice. Other programs send money overseas to support people with AIDS/

Protection from Discrimination

There are laws in the United States and Canada that make it illegal to discriminate against anyone on the basis of race, creed, color, and sex; these laws also ensure that people with HIV or AIDS are protected from discrimination. In 1990, the US Congress passed the Americans with Disabilities Act. This act specifically prohibits discrimination against anyone with HIV or AIDS.

That is the law. But in practice, there are still many ignorant people who are prejudiced against things they don't understand. HIV is scary enough without people treating each other badly.

You may see prejudice and discrimination happening. Sometimes you will be able to improve a situation right away. Sometimes your efforts will have more results if you work as part of a group, for education, justice, or one small improvement.

HIV or their orphaned children. There is an art exhibit of quilts designed to commemorate people with AIDS, called the AIDS Memorial Quilt, which tours North America.

The late Princess Diana was the first wife of Charles, the Prince of Wales. Photographers used to follow her almost everywhere because her husband was the heir to the British throne and also because she had become an icon in her own right. When visiting hospitals, Princess Diana would shake hands with people who had AIDS. Though photographers made her uncomfortable, she made sure that pictures were taken of these handshakes. Because her photographs appeared in many newspapers, she hoped this would help people understand that we don't have to be afraid to talk to and touch someone who has AIDS.

HIV is no longer a death sentence for those who receive the diagnosis. Stay positive!

Glossary

anonymous HIV testing A type of HIV testing in which the person tested is assigned a unique code that is used for identification instead of his or her name; the test results are completely confidential.

antibiotics Drugs used to treat infection.

antibody A substance made by a person's T cells to fight a particular infection.

asymptomatic Having an illness but without any symptoms.

bacteria Microscopic single-cell organisms, some of which can cause diseases.

blood transfusion The transfer of blood or blood products from one person to another.

CD4 count A test done to count the number of T cells in the immune system of a person with HIV or AIDS.

chemotherapy The treatment of cancer using drugs that are intended to destroy malignant cells.

contagious Able to be passed from one person to another.

dementia A significant decline in mental abilities, including memory loss and the ability to take care of one's self.

dental dam A square piece of latex usually used in dental procedures, but which can be used to practice safe sex.

diagnosis The identification of an illness.

DNA (deoxyribonucleic acid) The molecule inside the nucleus of a cell that carries the genetic instructions for making living organisms.

enzyme A protein that triggers chemical reactions in the body.

epidemic A widespread outbreak of an infectious disease.

GRID Gay-related immune deficiency; an early term used for the disease now called AIDS.

hemophilia A genetic condition from birth in which a person's blood does not clot properly, causing excessive bleeding from a slight injury.

HIV Human immunodeficiency virus; the virus that causes AIDS.

immune system The body's defense system against illness, disease, and infection.

intravenous drug use Directly injecting drugs into the bloodstream by using a needle.

Kaposi's sarcoma A rare type of cancer causing skin lesions.

lubricant An oily or slippery substance used to reduce friction and trauma during sexual intercourse.

lymph node A small gland that makes up part of the body's immune system that fights against invading bacteria and foreign particles.

lymphoma A cancer of the lymphatic system.

mutate To change, as in the genetic material of a cell.

opportunistic infection An infection that occurs when organisms take advantage of a weakened immune system.

PCP (pneumocystis carinii pneumonia) A form of pneumonia seen primarily in patients with weakened immune systems.

protease inhibitors A class of drugs that works to kill HIV when the virus is making copies of itself.

retrovirus A type of virus that has RNA.

For More Information

amfAR
120 Wall Street, 13th Floor
New York, NY 10005-3908
(212) 806-1600
Website: http://www.amfar.org
Facebook: @amfarthefoundationforaidsresearch
Twitter and Instagram: @amfar
AmfAR works to invest in finding a cure for AIDS.
    Since 1985, the organization has raised more
    than $517 million for AIDS research.

Avert
Website: http://www.avert.org
Email: info@avert.org
Facebook and Instagram: @avertAIDS
Twitter: @avert_org
This UK-based organization has been educating
    the public about HIV and AIDS for more than
    thirty years. Their website provides a wealth of
    information on HIV and living with the disease.

Canadian AIDS Society (CAS)
170 Laurier Avenue W, Suite 602
Ottawa, ON K1P 5V5

(800) 499-1986

Website: http://www.cdnaids.ca

Facebook: @aidsida

Twitter and Instagram: @cdnaids

CAS works with community-based HIV/AIDS organizations across Canada. They promote awareness, mobilize communities, and advocate public policy.

CATIE

555 Richmond Street West

Suite 505, Box 1104

Toronto, Ontario

M5V 3B1

Canada

(416) 203-7122

Email: questions@catie.ca

Website: http://www.catie.ca

Facebook and Twitter: @CATIEInfo

A Canadian source for HIV information, CATIE strives to keep up with the latest medical breakthroughs and to provide accurate, up-to-date, unbiased information about HIV.

HIV.gov
Office of HIV/AIDS and Infectious Disease
Policy (OHAIDP)
US Department of Health and Human Services
330 C Street SW, Room L100
Washington, DC 20024
Website: http://HIV.gov
Facebook, Twitter, and Instagram: @HIVgov
This website provides up-to-date information on
HIV, from living with the disease to current
medical protocols.

Ryan White HIV/AIDS Program
(301) 443-0493
Website: https://hab.hrsa.gov/about-ryan-white
-hivaids-program
This program helps to provide medical care and
support services for those living with HIV who
are uninsured or underinsured.

UNAIDS
20, Avenue Appia
CH-1211 Geneva 27
Switzerland

+ 41 22 791 36 66

Email: aidsinfo@unaids.org

http://www.unaids.org

Facebook and Twitter: @unaids

Instagram: @unaidsglobal

UNAIDS is a global organization working to end
the AIDS epidemic. It is cosponsored by the
Joint Programme in the United Nations.

For Further Reading

Czerwiec, MK. *Taking Turns: Stories from HIV/AIDS Care Unit 371*. University Park, PA: The Pennsylvania State University Press, 2017.

Dakers, Diane. *Magic Johnson: Basketball Legend, Entrepreneur, and HIV/AIDS Activist*. New York, NY: Crabtree Publishing, 2017.

Dicker, Katie. *AIDS and HIV*. New York, NY: Rosen Central, 2011.

Hopkins, Ellen. *Tilt*. New York, NY: Margaret K. McElderry Books, 2014.

Kallen, Stuart A. *The Race to Virus : Luc Montagnier vs. Robert Gallo*. Minneapolis, MN: Twenty-First Century Books, 2013.

Levithan, David. *Two Boys Kissing*. New York, NY: Ember, 2015.

Mantell, Paul. *Arthur Ashe: Young Tennis Champion*. New York, NY: Aladdin, 2014.

McPartland, Randall. *HIV and AIDS*. New York, NY: Cavendish Square, 2016.

Rawl, Paige. *Positive: Surviving My Bullies, Finding Hope, and Living to Change the World*. New York, NY: Harper, 2014.

Verdi, Jessica. *My Life After Now*. Naperville, IL: Sourcebooks Fire, 2013.

Bibliography

Avert. "Life expectancy for people with HIV is now near-normal—but only for those accessing treatment." May 15, 2017. https://www.avert .org/news/life-expectancy-people-hiv-now-near -normal-%E2%80%93-only-those-accessing -treatment.

Avert. "Using Condoms, Condom Types & Condom Sizes." August 2006 http://www.avert .org/usecond.htm. Retrieved November 1, 2018.

Division of HIV/AIDS Prevention. "Home Tests." National Center for HIV/AIDS, Viral Hepatitis, STD, and TB Prevention, October 6, 2015. https://www.cdc.gov/hiv/testing/hometests.html.

Division of HIV/AIDS Prevention. "Injection Drug Use and HIV Risk." National Center for HIV and AIDS, Centers for Disease Control and Prevention, August 3, 2018. https://www.cdc .gov/hiv/risk/idu.html.

Division of HIV/AIDS Prevention. "Oral Sex and HIV Risk." Centers for Disease Control and Prevention, July 8, 2016. https://www.cdc.gov /hiv/risk/oralsex.html.

Global AIDS Update. "Ending AIDS, Progress Toward the 90-90-90 Targets." UNAIDS

Retrieved October 23, 2018. http://www.unaids
.org/sites/default/files/media_asset
/Global_AIDS_update_2017_en.pdf.

Hahn, Jason Duaine. "Woman, 45, Who Was
Diagnosed with HIV at 18, Shares Her Powerful
Story: 'I Believe in Life.'" *People*, September 27,
2018. https://people.com/human-interest
/maria-mejia-hiv-aids-story.

Heisler, Mark. "Magic Johnson's career ended by
HIV-positive test. Lakers star says: 'I plan to go
on living for a long time.'" *LA Times*, November
7, 2016. http://www.latimes.com/sports
/lakers/la-sp-magic-johnson-hiv-test-archives
-20161107-story.html.

HIV/AIDS: Statistics Center. "HIV in the United
States: *At A Glance*." Centers for Disease Control
and Prevention, June 2018. https://www.cdc.
gov/hiv/pdf/statistics/overview/cdc-hiv-us
-ataglance.pdf.

HIV.gov, US Government Website. "What Can
You Expect When You Go in for an HIV
Test?" US Department of Health & Human
Services, May 14, 2018. https://www.hiv.gov
/hiv-basics/hiv-testing/learn-about-hiv
-testing/hiv-testing-overview.

HIV Risk Reduction Tool. "Stages of HIV
Infection." Centers for Disease Control and
Prevention. Retrieved October 24, 2018. https://
wwwn.cdc.gov/hivrisk/what_is/stages_hiv
_infection.html.

National Center for HIV/AIDS, Viral Hepatitis,
STD, and TB Prevention, Centers for Disease
Control and Prevention. "CDC Fact Sheet.
Today's HIV/AIDS Epidemic." August 2016.
https://www.cdc.gov/nchhstp/newsroom/docs
/factsheets/todaysepidemic-508.pdf

Scutti, Susan. "US teen birth rate drops to all
-time low." CNN, June 30, 2017. https://www
.cnn.com/2017/06/30/health/teen-birth-rate
-prenatal-care-2016/index.html.

UNAIDS. "Fact Sheet July 2018." July 2018. http://
www.unaids.org/sites/default/files/media_asset
/UNAIDS_FactSheet_en.pdf.

US Department of Health and Human Services.
"FDA-Approved HIV Medicines." September 4,
2018. https://aidsinfo.nih.gov/understanding
-hiv-aids/fact-sheets/21/58/fda-approved-hiv
-medicines.

US Department of Health and Human Services.
July 2006. "HIV and Its Treatment: What You

Should Know. Health Information for Patients," US Department of Justice. "Questions and Answers: The Americans with Disabilities Act and Persons with HIV/AIDS." August 2006. https://www.ada.gov/hiv/ada_q&a_aids.htm.

Index

About the Authors

Elissa Thompson is a journalist who has been published in *USA Weekend*, the *Baltimore Sun*, and *In Touch Weekly*, among other publications. She received her master's in journalism from the University of Maryland and has worked on other books for Rosen Publishing, including *Coping with Stress*.

Paula Johanson has worked for twenty years as a writer and teacher, and she has written and edited educational materials for the Alberta Distance Learning Centre in Canada. She writes and edits nonfiction books, magazine articles and columns, and book reviews. She has been nominated twice for the national Prix Aurora Award for Canadian Science Fiction. She had a blood transfusion in early 1985, before AIDS/HIV screening, but took an HIV test as soon as it was available. Johanson lives on an island in British Columbia and a farm in Alberta, Canada.

Photo Credits

Cover The Times/Gallo Images/Getty Images; p. 5 Smith Collection /Gado/Archive Photos/Getty Images; p. 6 Stephen Dunn/Getty Images; p. 7 Aris Messinis/AFP/Getty Images; p. 11 Steve Gschmeissner /Science Photo Library/Getty Images; p. 15 asiseeit/E+/Getty Images; p. 17 Andrew Brookes/Cultura/Getty Images; p. 19 Tina Stallard /Getty Images; p. 23 Jill Giardino/Blend Images/Getty Images; p. 28 © iStockphoto/Vasyl Dolmatov; p. 32 © iStockphoto/DMEPhotography; p. 34 Kim Komenich/The LIFE Images Collection/Getty Images; p. 39 LAGUNA DESIGN/Science Photo Library/Getty Images; p. 42 © iStockphoto/dusanpetkovic; p. 47 Francis Sheehan/Science Source; p. 51 © iStockphoto/jarun011; p. 57 Phanie/Alamy Stock Photo; p. 60 digitalskillet/iStock/Getty Images; p. 65 Alexander Raths/Shutterstock .com; p. 69 © iStockphoto/utah778; p. 71 Nataly Studio/Shutterstock.com; p. 75 Nik Panisov/Shutterstock.com; p. 79 Hero Images/Getty Images; p. 81 Barbara Neveu/Shutterstock.com; p. 84 Vstock LLC/Getty Images; p. 90 © iStockphoto/Ridofranz.

Design and Layout: Nicole Russo-Duca; Photo Researcher: Karen Huang